G000109551

How To Hide A

HANG OVER

ALLSORTED.

An exclusive edition for

ALLSORTED.
for all your gift books and gift stationery

This edition published in Great Britain in 2020
by Allsorted Ltd, Watford, Herts, UK WD19 4BG

© Susanna Geoghegan Gift Publishing

Author: Michael Powell
Design: Milestone Creative
Layout: seagulls.net

ISBN: 978-1-912295-23-4

Printed in China

How To Hide A
HANG
OVER

★ & OTHER COOL WAYS TO ★

BEHAVE BADLY

CONTENTS

HOW *TO* Hide a HANGOVER

One of the main reasons that a hangover is difficult to hide – apart from panda eyes, the dry heaving, yesterday's clothes, the feeling that a small furry animal just died in your mouth, electrolyte and vitamin depletion, the urge to crawl under your desk, self-loathing and a lingering low-level paranoia – is dehydration.

The lack of H_2O is the reason everyone will know you've had a night on the lash. A hangover will give you a pounding skull, cause sleepiness, a raging thirst and dry skin. Do you also have a puffy face? That's caused by water retention, as your body frantically tries to plug the leaks, since you spent the last three hours peeing like a puppy with a urinary tract infection.

To stand any hope of feeling and looking marginally better than subhuman, drink lots of water. Take frequent ostentatious glugs from a large plastic bottle, and blend in with all the other high-functioning alcoholics hiding in plain sight with whom you have blithely shared an office without realising that these smug Evian-toting colleagues aren't vegan health nuts – they're homeless boozehounds like you, and they sleep in their cars.

Once you've nailed the water loss/retention conundrum, you can address the 'redface'. That Deadpool vibe is a major giveaway, caused by acetaldehyde (ethanal) which is what you get when your body partially breaks down all the alcohol (ethanol) by removing just two tiny hydrogen atoms. This causes your hangover, and triggers the release of histamine in your body, which gives you flushed cheeks.

Pop some anti-histamines and use some concealer, or better still, take the amino acid L-cysteine before getting wasted. It lowers levels of acetaldehyde in the body – especially in the stomach – when you get bladdered. The ethanal is eventually broken down into relatively harmless acetic acid. The best way to mimic the morning after without hitting your wallet or raising your cancer risk, is to abstain and then shotgun a bottle of malt vinegar for breakfast.

SEVEN WAYS TO
Remain Cool when You're
BLADDERED

**We all want to look cool,
but not at the expense of being
stone cold sober, right?**

So how do you become the coolest person in the room while still being mashed off your face?

1. Stand/sit up straight. Good posture gives you a strong presence, and sends out the message that you are confident and respect yourself. That doesn't mean stiffening up like you've just had spinal surgery. Imagine a string attached to the top of your head, and someone is gently pulling it upwards. Relax your neck, breathe easily

and without actually doing anything, imagine your back is lengthening and widening. Maintaining your posture is hard when you're drunk, especially when you're bent over trying not to puke on your shoes.

2. Wear clothes that still work for you when you're mullered. Don't get drunk in a suit (unless it's unavoidable, e.g. before a court appearance or during a wake), because suits are for sober people. Drunk people in suits look and act like proper idiots. You can't maintain that crisp, freshly laundered look when you're legless, but you could still rock a sheer black cocktail dress or a leather jacket and a pair of Wayfarer sunglasses. However, don't make the mistake of choosing clothes that are already associated with drinking culture, such as a Hawaiian shirt, toga, rugby or football shirt.

3. Don't attempt to eat anything. It's a dead giveaway. You may think you're negotiating that finger buffet with sober finesse, but scoffing 42 miniature Scotch eggs and then using a wedge of pizza to scoop up an entire bowl of hummus, doesn't cut the mustard. Also, that damp cushion you just sat on? It was a plate of vegetarian quesadillas.

DON'T GET DRUNK IN A SUIT

4. Don't be tempted to pick up a guitar, even if you're really good.

The assembled company don't want to spend two hours pretending to enjoy your Ed Sheeran covers.

5. Instead of talking crap, become a good listener. Nature gave you one tongue and two ears, but alcohol gives most people a big flappy word hole at the bottom of their face, and the unshakeable belief that their random unfiltered thoughts can usher in the next great leap in human evolution.

6. You know that giant kebab that you're going to devour on the way home and can't stop talking about? It's a good plan, but not an interesting topic of conversation. Read the room. Is anyone else riffing about yoghurt sauce right now?

7. Drunk people are like: IDGAF; genuinely cool people are the same, only in a good way. Don't confuse the two.

A man walks into a bar pushing a wheelbarrow, which contains a large piece of tarmac. 'What can I get you?' asks the bartender. 'A beer please, and one for the road.'

How to DRINK WHISKY

A hoary pseudo-culture is as synonymous with spirits as the giant seagulls that pervade the streets and skies of Aberdeen, but whisky seems to attract more than its fair share of ritual and self-styled aficionados, who hold forth about the correct way to drink it.

In Scotland, if you ask for ice or water with your whisky, expect to receive the disdainful retort, 'bite me ye radge wee lump'. Whisky takes its wholesome name from the Scottish Gaelic word 'uisge beatha' which means 'water of life', suggesting that it's vital for survival, or that life isn't worth living without it. Meanwhile, no one can even agree on its spelling.

DRINKING WHISKY IS REALLY QUITE SIMPLE

Malt whisky is made primarily from malted grain; grain whisky is made from any type of grain, while blended malt whisky is a combination of several single malts from different distilleries. A single malt is made in one distillery using one particular malted grain; cask strength (aka barrel proof) is high quality and bottled undiluted from the cask; and single cask is bottled from an individual barrel, so the quality will vary from cask to cask, even within the same brand.

Even though the choice can be daunting, drinking whisky is really quite simple; if anyone tells you otherwise and you've had a wee dram, speak confidently in the vernacular: 'yer bum's oot the windae, ye fecking bampot'.

Take the Taste Test

First, take a look at the colour, which can range from a coppery yellow to a golden red. This gives you clues about how the whisky was made. In general, the longer it spends in the oak barrel, the closer its hue will be to the cauliflower nose of a Tobermory trawlerman. Cheaper whisky gain the same effect by adding caramel colouring.

Second, swill the liquid around the glass and watch how it drips back down the sides into the body (these drips are called 'legs'). The lighter and younger the whisky, the more quickly the legs will run back; the legs on an older, heavier-bodied whisky take longer to run back and are more viscous or oily. A really thick, old whisky will cling to the sides of the glass like the lipids lining the artery walls of a Glaswegian welder.

Third, keeping your mouth slightly open, stick your nose in the glass and have a good sniff to appreciate all the subtle aromas. At first you might only sense a hit of alcohol, but the more you practise, the more you'll be able to detect.

Finally, take a sip, hold it in your mouth for a few seconds (chew it a little if that helps you to sense the flavours) and then swallow. At this moment, if you were a hard-drinking cowboy in a movie, you'd wipe your mouth on your sleeve, slam the shot glass back on the counter and nod for a refill. Don't do this ('you lavvy-headed lump'); simply savour the whisky's 'finish' – see how long the warmth stays with you.

Adding a little water is allowed, as it helps to unlock the flavour in some brands whisky, while adding ice tends to lock up the flavour. Do whatever suits your taste and makes you feel warm and fuzzy.

ADDING A LITTLE WATER IS ALLOWED

Wake Up and
PASS THE PORT,
YOU DOZY ARSE

Port wine is a sweet, heavy, 'fortified' red wine made in Portugal in the Douro Valley.

Port is often called a dessert wine because of its sweetness, but it can be drunk as an aperitif. It has a higher alcohol content than normal wine (about 20 per cent versus 11 to 14 per cent) because distilled grape spirits such as brandy are added, which halts fermentation. This means that not all of the sugar turns into alcohol, which accounts for the sweeter taste.

Port is best appreciated when drunk using small sips. Tawny and Reserve Port should be served at just below room temperature, around 10 to 16°C, while Rosé and White Port should be a colder 4 to 10°C. After the port has been decanted, the decanter is traditionally placed on the table to the right of the host. Its passage around a table is then governed by the usual sphincter-tightening etiquette posh people devise to embellish their vices.

The host unstoppers the decanter and, instead of serving himself, he uses his left hand to pass it to the person on his left, who pours himself a drink and then passes to his left, using his left hand, and so forth until the port arrives back at the host, who finally pours his own drink, re-stoppers the decanter and then declares a toast. The port must always be passed to the left, never right or across the table, and no one must take a sip until the host has made the toast. A lady should not touch or pour the port; that is the duty of the gentleman to her right.

If the decanter comes to a standstill during its clockwise journey around the table, it's considered bad form to ask directly for it. Instead, you should politely enquire of the tardy diner to your right, 'Do you know the Bishop of Norwich?' which should tactfully get the decanter moving again. This practice dates back to 1837 when the Right Reverend Henry Bathurst, Bishop of Norwich, aged 93, developed a reputation for falling asleep at the dinner table.

Passing to the left is often wrongly associated with the red 'port' navigation light on a British naval ship, though British naval officers were passing port to the left as early as the late eighteenth century.

DRINK ALL DAY *Without Getting* SLEEPY

Drinking all day can be a transcendent experience, sitting in the morning sun, still seated when the evening comes, wasting time.

Nothing beats a lazy day of placid boozing, but like any endurance event, it takes preparation and a little common sense. These tips will help you to keep your end up:

1. Clear your diary. This will only work if you pick a genuinely guilt-free day, with no commitments, deadlines, children or tasks; just eighteen hours of leisure time stretching ahead like an undeviating highway through wide-open prairie that dissolves into shallow purple hills where an

azure sky meets the horizon. No criticism or passive aggression from family members or household tasks to squeeze in before nightfall, just unsullied drinking with a couple of like-minded friends.

2. Make sure you've slept well – booze free – the night before. If you're tired and hung-over, you'll flake out in the middle of the afternoon and wake up early evening with a killer headache (stop baulking, Ernest Hemingway, one day off the booze won't kill you).

3. Leave your mobile phone at home. Today you'll be uncontactable, unplugged, off the grid. You're JD Salinger, Lauryn Hill, The Wachowskis, Harper Lee.

4. Before you head out to the beer garden of your chosen drinking establishment, have a hearty breakfast, mixing complex carbohydrates like oatmeal or whole-wheat toast, with a big greasy fry-up, then keep eating and snacking throughout the day. You're an artisan. You can't do this on an empty stomach.

5. Stay out of the sun. Sit watching the ships roll out and away, but do it in the shade. Sun and booze go together like mosquitoes and citronella candles. A famous Impressionist artist used to spend all

YOU
CAN'T DO
THIS ON A
AN EMPTY
STOMACH

day in the sun drinking Absinthe on an empty stomach. Sounds idyllic doesn't it? His name was Vincent van Gogh.

6. Start with your three favourite drinks. The key to the rest of the day will be pacing yourself, so if neat vodka is your thing, get it on board early and really appreciate settling into your buzz, so that later you can happily commit to a pragmatic transition to the long haul.

7. Stay hydrated. Aim to have one glass of water for every alcoholic drink you consume. In Italy, everyone sensibly alternates between booze and coffee (which doesn't improve their stagnating economy, organised crime and rampant youth unemployment).

8. Don't get into slamming shots or competitive drinking. Enjoy making each alcoholic drink last an hour, and pretend it's the last one before you check into rehab.

9. If at any time throughout the day you feel dizzy or even close to spewing, slow down. This is a marathon, remember? Don't be the loser whose legs turn into trombones after twenty-two miles so that a first-responder has to carry you over the finish line like a new-born baby deer. This is your own private Idaho and you're damn well staying the course.

"*Drink because you are happy, but never because you are miserable.*"

G.K. CHESTERTON, *HERETICS*

DRINK
*** *Champagne* ***
LIKE THE FRENCH

Here is a typically Gallic meander from viticulture to palate, since the French probably have a famous saying: 'anticipation is the best part of any pleasure'.

Only the sparkling wine made using traditional methods in the northwestern Champagne region of France, from specific types of local grapes (primarily Pinot noir, Pinot meunier and Chardonnay as well as small amounts of Pinot blanc, Pinot gris, Arbane and Petit Meslier) can legally call itself 'Champagne', as designated by the Treaty of Madrid in 1891.

A handful of sparkling wine producers in the United States still manage to get away with calling their bubbly 'Champagne' and the village of Champagne in Switzerland has manufactured a still wine called 'Champagne' since the seventeenth century, but the Swiss government phased out

IF YOU WANT THE GENUINE ARTICLE, IT HAS TO BE FRENCH

the name in the early twenty-first century. Basically, if you want the genuine article, it has to be French – they've been making fizzy wine since the fifth century.

Next, you must learn how to store, chill and open the bottle. Champagne is best stored on its side in a cool dark place – the fridge is fine for a few days, but not long-term, because it will dry out the cork, making it shrink, breaking the seal and allowing the contents to oxidise. The best way to chill your Champers from room temperature is to place the bottle in an ice bucket filled with ice and one-third water for 20 minutes. The ideal serving temperature is around 10°C.

When removing the cork, loosen the metal cage but don't remove it completely, as this allows you to control the cork as you twist the bottle (not the cork) and then open discretely. Avoid at all costs a loud pop and accompanying foam-fest: reserve those vulgarities for the Formula One podium or the end of a U2 concert. Don't even think about using a sword – 'sabrage' is for good reason an anagram of 'arsebag'.

Champagne is traditionally poured into a narrow flute glass, but a white wine glass is preferable, as it allows you to better enjoy the complex aromas. Only fill a third of the glass, otherwise the champagne will warm up too quickly. Also, hold the glass by the stem, not the bowl, for the same reason.

Et alors, nous voilà: take a fragrant sniff followed by your first sip! Pair with oysters and caviar, truffle fries, canapés, *fromage* or whatever else floats your *bateau* and launch into an evening of subtle *recherche du plaisir*.

> A woman walks into a bar and orders 10 separate shots of neat vodka. After the bartender has lined them up, the woman pours away the first and the last shots. 'Why did you do that?' asks the bartender. 'Oh, because the first always tastes horrible and the last one makes me sick.'

GET SERVED
when You're
TOO DRUNK

Sometimes the law can be a giant hypocritical arse, and never more so than when applied to alcohol sales.

It's acceptable to serve someone enough alcohol to make them drunk, but then once they *are* drunk, it's illegal to sell them anymore. That's rather like pushing your car off a cliff and then blaming the ground for the damage because it was fine while it was coasting through the air.

Anyway, this means that when you're bladdered, you'll only get served if you can fight the effects of alcohol and appear sober. Short of a blood transfusion, there's nothing you can do to bring down your blood alcohol level, but you can slow down its increase by eating a meal to reduce the speed at which the alcohol in the next drink enters your bloodstream. Also, drink a pint of water, because dehydration will increase your impairment. Coffee will also make you feel momentarily more alert, but it takes 40 minutes for the caffeine to reach your bloodstream.

Go outside and get some fresh air. This will make you feel instantly more alert. Next, open your eyes. Drunk people have droopy eyes. If your eyes are bloodshot, use some witch hazel eye drops (if you can tilt your head back without falling over). Try not to squirt the drops up your nose. Your eyes will magically become bright white again, momentarily, ready for you to approach the bar.

Keep your head up and take deep calming breaths as you walk briskly to the bar and then as you cling on to it for support, employ the minimum of words to order. Slurred speech is a dead giveaway. Speak slowly and clearly, and try to formulate sentences that require little tongue tip articulation.

If you're ordering a pint, take a sip before you walk away, so you're less likely to spill any. If you've ordered a round, make two trips. Don't risk using a tray.

Don't be all serious, but don't try to smile. Even the most innocent drunken smile is only a whisker away from looking totally bladdered. You may think you appear warm and charming, but actually you look like you just drank the whole bar.

"*I don't have a drinking problem 'cept when I can't get a drink.*"

TOM WAITS

WHY *** Safe Units are RUBBISH

The safe level of units of alcohol is so variable around the world that in some countries you could drink enough booze in a single day to exceed the weekly limit elsewhere.

There's no official World Health Organization guidance, so individual countries have made up their own figures. The amount of alcohol you can safely drink depends on your gender, where you live and whether you have access to a time machine.

Australia recommends no more than 28 units a week (a 175 ml glass of wine at 13 per cent ABV is around 2.3

units) and the US official guideline is 14 units a week, but in 1979, the maximum alcohol weekly intake in the UK was a staggering 56 units a week of alcohol. By 2016, this had been reduced to 14 units a week for men and women, with the warning that there's no safe level of drinking. Today in Guyana, the recommended maximum intake is 7 units of alcohol a week, but in Fiji it's 52 units of alcohol a week. Continental Europe is between these two extremes, with 35/22 units of alcohol a week (male/female) in Spain and 26/17 units of alcohol a week in France.

In the USA, an estimated 88,000 people (approximately 62,000 men and 26,000 women) die from excessive alcohol use each year, making alcohol the third leading preventable cause of death (after tobacco and poor diet/physical inactivity). But there are approximately 2.625 million deaths each year in the US, so you might consider 3.35 per cent of deaths from alcohol abuse quite low, especially compared with the 40,000 people who are shot dead. So, is the alcohol mortality rate restricted to those super messed-up winos who drink three bottles of vodka a day? Surely it doesn't apply to your single-bottle-of-wine-every-evening habit?

WARNING: THERE'S NO SAFE LEVEL OF DRINKING!

It's common knowledge that moderate drinking is better than being teetotal, but when you look at studies comparing the mortality of drinkers to non-drinkers, in some models a drinker can consume 50 units a week before he or she surpasses the mortality level of a teetotaller. Your government kept that finding quiet, didn't they?

A bottle a day...

A recent UK study published in the journal *BMC Public Health*, estimated the cancer risk of a bottle of wine as equivalent to five cigarettes for men and ten for women per week. So, a man would have to drink two bottles of wine a day to have the same cancer risk as a ten-a-day male smoker.

It's tempting to think that being a high functioning alcohol dependent is relatively safe, so long as your intake doesn't creep up to park-bench-sleeper-wino levels, and you may be right. Maybe excess alcohol won't kill you prematurely, but do bear in mind that one bottle of wine a night can still ruin your marriage, your relationship with your children, hurt your wallet, lower your productivity and turn you into a sad fat sack.

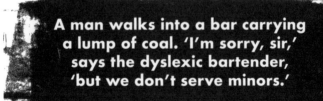

A man walks into a bar carrying a lump of coal. 'I'm sorry, sir,' says the dyslexic bartender, 'but we don't serve minors.'

Drink VODKA Like a Russian

We've all seen the films – a semi-circle of Russians in trench coats gruffly shout 'Nostrovia!', down their vodka shots in unison and then fling the empty glasses into the fire. Oh, if only it were that simple.

In fact, the etiquette associated with Russian vodka drinking is as intricate and colourful as that painted gingerbread cathedral in Red Square. First of all, modern Russians don't drink as much as the previous generations, and many don't

29

drink at all. But if you're a traditionalist, these drinking rules still apply:

1. If you turn up late, your drinking companions may require you to drink a penalty shot. This tradition originated with Peter the Great, who made his tardy subordinates down a 1.5 litre glass of vodka in one.

2. The second glass of vodka follows swiftly after the first, and on no account should you eat anything in between.

3. 'Nostrovia!' isn't a toast. It's used to thank someone for a meal or drink. The most common Russian toast is 'За здоровье!' [za zda-ró-vye], which means 'your health!'. Variations on this toast which also mean 'your health!' include 'Ваше здоровье!' [vashee zda-ró-vye], 'Твоё здоровье!' [tva-jó zda-ró-vye] (informal). 'Будем здоровы!' [bóo-deem zda-ró-vye"] means 'to our health!'

4. Toasting health is just the start. A new toast should be pronounced every time a glass is raised, otherwise it's a sign you may have a drinking problem. During a typical liver-scarring session, you can expect to toast everything from friendship 'За нашу дружбу!' [za ná-shoo dróo-zhboo] to the peaceful sky above your head 'За мирное небо над головой!' [Za mirnoye nebo nad golovoi].

5. As soon as the vodka has been poured, you should remove the bottle from the table. This old Cossack tradition, from the time of the Napoleonic Wars, was a way of reducing the tab in drinking establishments by secreting empty bottles under the table.

6. The same person should pour a single bottle of vodka; if the pourer is changed mid-bottle, superstition warns that a drunken fight will break out.

7. When a guest is ready to leave a party, the host usually proposes one last drink for the road – 'На посошок!' [na pa-sa-shók] In times past, the guest would be required to neck this final 'breathalyser' glass while it was balanced on the handle of a walking stick. If the glass fell, the guest was obliged to remain, rather than risk a bad journey.

A lion walks into a bar and asks for a job. 'No, sorry,' replies the manager, 'but the circus is in town, why don't you try them?' The lion shrugs and says, 'Why would the circus need a bartender?'

Get Served in a CROWDED BAR

Nothing can ruin your drinking fun more quickly than standing at a crowded bar trying to catch the attention of the bar staff, wishing you were a foot taller and wondering if you've unwittingly developed the superpower of invisibility.

Fortunately, there are a few things you can do to increase your chances of getting served.

First, some don'ts: don't wave your money around, snap your fingers or indignantly tell the server that it's your turn next. You may even be right, but you're still wrong, and rudeness or anger will bump you to the back of the queue. In fact, allowing someone else to get served ahead of you doesn't go unnoticed, and can ensure that you're next.

You may not be tall, but you can still use your body language to attract attention. Research shows that the best tactic is to stand squarely to the bar with your head facing forward and to focus all your attention on the barperson as they move around, so that you can catch their eye when they are ready to serve the next person. If you squeeze in sideways, you take up less space and physically demand less attention. Also, if you're distracted by talking to your friends or looking around, you'll also miss the opportunity to lock eyes with the server. If you're distracted, there's less urgency for the server to satisfy your order, because only those who are actively bidding for attention (without being rude) get served quickly. You actually have to appear eager and attentive, but not irritable or angry.

Raise your eyebrows, smile and look amenable. It makes you more appealing to serve. No one wants to serve the angry frowning customer who looks like they are going to give the server a stream of abuse.

It also pays to stand as close as possible to the till, because the servers have to go there frequently, and are more likely to be in your sight line.

When you've finally been served, tip generously and you'll be remembered the next time. Even if this is your final visit to the bar, tip anyway. Working in the service industry is hard, low paid work.

MIXING YOUR DRINKS: *Mixologist or* PISSHEAD?

Mixology is the art of inventing, preparing and serving mixed drinks or cocktails; mixing your drinks is something entirely different. Never confuse the two.

Blending two or more alcoholic drinks in a glass is a skill; mixing them together in your stomach can be a recipe for the biggest hangover of your life, although it's a case of correlation rather than causation.

The old folk wisdom says, 'Grape or grain, but never the twain' and 'beer before liquor, never been sicker; liquor before beer, you're in the clear'. Mixing your drinks is reputed to be bad because of certain 'congeners' (compounds produced during the manufacturing process, of which as a rule of thumb, darker drinks are supposed to contain more), but in fact, research has shown that they have little effect on levels of intoxication or hangovers.

The main reason that mixing your drinks makes you pay the next morning is that people who mix their drinks have often had too much already. The more you drink, the worse you are at judging how much you've drunk.

The 'beer before liquor' saying is only true because beer is lower in alcohol than wine or spirits, so if you switch from beer when you're already drunk, you're more likely to knock the wine or spirits back more quickly, rather than sip more slowly. Although carbonated drinks irritate the stomach lining, and tend to marginally increase the rate of alcohol absorption.

Mixing energy drinks with alcohol is a really bad move. The caffeine they contain helps you to feel less drunk, which can encourage you to drink more and postpone the ill effects until the following morning. Research shows that people who mix energy drinks with alcohol have a higher risk of injury from fights and car accidents than those who just drink alcohol (but that may just be because they represent a more feral and aggressive sub group).

Ultimately, the only relevant factors are the total units of alcohol and the rate at which they are metabolised (dictated by the rate of consumption and stomach contents, i.e. drinking with food means the alcohol reaches the bloodstream more slowly).

Recently, gin has enjoyed its biggest surge in popularity since the Gin Craze which overran London in the first half of the eighteenth century.

Modern hipster gin drinkers aren't the feckless alcoholics depicted in William Hogarth's famous engraving, *Gin Lane*; today it's all about the beards, botanicals and fancy tonics.

This 'gintrification' is a fantastic opportunity for hardened drinkers, because the more you bone up on the subtle flavour combinations, the less chance anyone can accuse you of being a raging alcoholic. Whisky and wine bibbers know this well. For centuries, they've disguised their problem drinking as highbrow connoisseurship, but at the end of the day, it all goes down the same way and gives your liver a good lashing. So, buy a beanie hat and some oversized spectacles, tie your hair in a half bun and get your arse down to the supermarket to hunt for some botanical-heavy brands.

If you're a newbie gin drinker, buy a small bottle of Gordon's London Dry Gin as your baseline. This triple-distilled old classic has been around since 1769, with its frugal handful of botanicals which include juniper (without the pine-flavoured juniper berries, it can't be called gin), coriander seeds, angelica root, liquorice, orris root, orange and lemon peel. Next, move on to a Bombay Sapphire, another old classic with 10 botanicals: those listed above (minus the orange peel), plus grains of Paradise, cubeb berries, cassia bark and almonds.

Then pull up some Wagner on your iTunes playlist and spend the rest of the day (because naturally you started drinking in the morning) hitting the Monkey 47 Schwarzwald Dry Gin from the Black Forest in Germany, which is not only 47 per cent proof, but has 47 different botanicals packed inside. You'll probably have to drink an entire bottle to spot them all. The botanicals are a bit of a gimmick, but reserve judgement until after you've tasted this robust, complex and reassuringly heavy masterpiece that comes in a no-nonsense brown medicine-style bottle.

You'll never take gin for granted again, and you'll learn in one single drinking session that there's a whole world of amazing gins out there for you to experience and – lucky you – this is just the beginning of your odyssey.

Am I an *

ALCOHOLIC?

Alcoholism – alcohol addiction, also known as 'alcohol use disorder' takes many forms, and is fiendishly difficult to self-diagnose, especially after a skinful.

In contrast, having a drinking problem or dependence is easily spotted – if alcohol causes you problems in your life, you have an alcohol problem, also known as alcohol abuse, which is a pattern of behaviour where a person drinks excessively in spite of the annoying people in their life nagging them to quit. Many of us will willingly admit to this lesser condition, but the problem with alcoholism is that acknowledgement is invariably an admission that the drinking has to stop, and that's difficult when reality is so messed up.

Several clinical alcohol assessment quizzes will tell you whether you're an alcoholic, with about 90 per cent accuracy (e.g. the CAGE test, the MAST quiz, the WHO's AUDIT alcohol assessment). These will give you a very reliable indicator of your potential alcoholism. However, as a preface, if these signs are a familiar pattern in your life, you're certainly far along the well-trodden path:

1. Talking utter crap in the pub for four hours with your mates is considered healthy social drinking, while drinking alone at home or in secrecy (e.g. hiding alcohol, lying about consumption) is a sign of problem drinking (sorry, but we don't make the rules).

2. Craving alcohol is bad; needing a drink is a sign of alcohol dependence (rather than the sane 'seeking retreat from a world gone mad').

3. Prioritising drinking over/neglecting responsibilities (if you hate your job or you're rubbish at DIY, naturally throwing a sickie and drinking five pints is a more attractive alternative).

4. Extreme mood swings and irritability (especially when friends and family tell you you're drinking too much).

CRAVING ALCOHOL IS BAD

5. Feelings of guilt associated with drinking (which you wouldn't have if people would just leave you alone).

6. Drinking first thing in the morning (OK, that's pretty serious, especially if the corner shop doesn't open until 9 a.m.).

7. Inability to stop or control your alcohol consumption (made worse by the drinks you have to bolt in secret).

8. Alcohol withdrawal symptoms (sweating, shakes, existential crisis, spare cash, etc.) – indicative of physical addiction.

9. Taking risks and breaking the law while intoxicated (although surely, breaking the law while sober is much naughtier).

10. Your drinking causes relationship problems (unless your partner drinks more than you).

11. Piss stains around the toilet bowl and a half-eaten kebab on the kitchen table.

12. High tolerance of bad conversation/music/television.

"First you take a drink, then the drink takes a drink, then the drink takes you."

F. SCOTT FITZGERALD, *THE GREAT GATSBY*

***

DRINK RUM
LIKE A PIRATE

Rum is a distilled alcoholic drink made from molasses or from sugarcane juice by a process of fermentation and distillation.

The clear distillate is then usually aged in oak barrels, where it acquires its distinctive deep brown colour.

The origin of the word rum is widely disputed. Some argue that it was taken from the last syllable for the Latin word for sugar, *saccharum*. Others credit an old British slang term for 'the best', as in 'having a rum time', or a truncated version of rumbullion or rumbustion, or even the Romany word rum, meaning 'strong' or 'potent'. It could even relate to the earliest rum distillers – Greek Christians in the eastern Mediterranean, since Rum is the Turkish name for Greeks.

Rum has long been associated with seafaring types. Men on long-haul sailing expeditions needed a way to keep the drinking water from going stagnant, so mixing it with alcohol was a luxury born of necessity. Until as recently as 1970, sailors in the Royal Navy received a daily rum ration (called a tot).

Pirates consumed their rum in a drink called bumbo by mixing it with water, sugar and nutmeg or cinnamon. That's your basic pirate bumbo drink, which probably wouldn't sit well with your millennial palate, so here's a modern take on the old pirate recipe:

    2 fluid oz dark rum
    1 fluid oz lemon juice
    ½ tsp Grenadine
    ¼ tsp (grated) nutmeg

Half fill a cocktail shaker with ice cubes, combine the ingredients and shake. Then strain into a cocktail glass, with a sugared rim. As you raise your glass aloft, pull a big toothless grin and yell, 'splice the main brace'. If your drinking pals look confused, explain to them that in days of yore, when sailors were ordered to perform the skilled and dangerous task of repairing the longest line of all the running rigging, they would be rewarded with extra rum rations; so the term has long been associated with getting bladdered at sea.

How to Fight when You're

DRUNK

**Getting into a fight is always a big mistake,
but fighting when drunk is borderline suicidal.**

Alcohol destroys your fighting prowess in many ways. It impairs your judgement and lowers your inhibitions, so that you overestimate your own abilities and underestimate those of your opponent.

Your drunken brain remembers that you've watched dozens of one punch ownage videos on YouTube, and persuades you to do a haymaker or roundhouse kick, despite the fact that you've never done either even sober. Alcohol also destroys your coordination, making your punches and kicks inaccurate and less powerful, and it slows down your defensive moves as well (although when have you ever seen a drunk person use defence?).

Tell you something you don't know, right? That's all self-evident when you're sober, so why can't you remember these indisputable facts when you've had a few drinks, and walk away from a fight? Alcohol is a powerful reality-altering drug. It makes people believe things that are manifestly untrue.

We've established that you're an idiot for fighting when drunk, but if you can't escape or talk your way out of the situation when you've had a skinful, follow these four rules:

1. Only fight people who are drunker than you. If your opponent is sober, insist on buying them a few drinks before 'taking it outside'.

2. Always hit first (while your opponent is nursing the pint or opening the packet of nuts you just bought them). Don't wait for your change.

3. Don't think about inflicting pain, because your opponent may be too drunk to feel very much. Concentrate on exploiting their impaired judgement by encouraging them to perform a choreographed dance move, sing karaoke, impulse buy something on Amazon or overshare on social media, then incapacitate with a basic choke hold.

4. Even if you 'win' the fight (which will typically last about 20 seconds), you'll still look like an arsehole. Remember this one if you're ever tempted to fight for your 'honour'.

WHAT KIND OF

*** Beer Belly ***

DO YOU HAVE?

When it comes to being overweight, men are luckier than women because they tend to carry most of their excess weight in the stomach.

Although this is worse for their health than storing fat uniformly, or around the hips and arse, it makes it easier for a fat man to look in the mirror, ignore his bulging belly, stare at his spindly legs and pretend he is thinner than his reflection tells him. So, it's better for the ego, but worse for the life expectancy.

Did you know that there are two types of beer belly? If your belly is big and wobbly, it may feel uncomfortable, but this is subcutaneous fat, which means it's deposited between the skin and the abdominal muscles. That's the best sort of beer belly to have. In most people, about 90 per cent of body fat is subcutaneous.

The other type of beer belly is firm to touch, doesn't jiggle much and can't be pinched. This means that most of this 'visceral' fat is stored inside the abdominal cavity, behind your abs, in the spaces between your vital organs, compressing the heart and lungs, liver and intestines, making them work harder. Visceral fat is associated with a number of health risks, including cardiovascular disease and type 2 diabetes. This is not just because of the cramped conditions inside your body; fat cells are biologically active – they form part of the endocrine system – and visceral fat particularly secretes hormones and other molecules which are linked to inflammation and insulin resistance.

If your belly is wobbly, don't feel too smug, because you may have lots of visceral fat plus big and wobbly subcutaneous belly fat. Weight loss programmes often stress the benefit of losing just 10 per cent of your body weight. This is because, not only does it make you feel better, but it also gets rid of up to 40 per cent of your visceral fat. So, a 10 per cent loss of body weight significantly improves your health prospects.

* Bar Tricks *

YOU DON'T HAVE TO BE

PISSED

* to Enjoy *

Most bar tricks are only barely
tolerable when everyone is
too drunk to hold a proper
conversation and some idiot with
inexplicably high self-esteem sees
it as his or her duty (usually his) to
entertain the assembled company.
But these three little beauties are
too good not to share.

1. Turn water into whisky

Your challenge: to swap the contents of two glasses without using a third receptacle.

Fill two shot glasses right to the top, one with whisky and the other with water. Place a thin beer mat (or playing card) tightly over the rim of the glass of water, then tip it upside down and place it on top of the glass of whisky so that the two rims are perfectly aligned. Then carefully slide the beer mat away slightly, to create a tiny chink of space where the two liquids can meet. The water will flow down into the bottom glass as the vacuum it leaves behind sucks all the whisky up into the top glass.

2. Olive in your martini

Your challenge: to place a single olive on a coaster and then add it to a martini glass without touching the glass, the olive or the coaster.

Place another empty wine glass over the olive and start swizzling it in a circle until you build up enough centrifugal force so that the olive sticks to the inside, then keep swizzling as you turn the glass upright. Once you've captured the olive, simply tip it into the martini.

START SWIZZLING IN A CIRCLE

3. Your buddy guesses the right card from a different city

Your challenge: phone a friend and they'll pick the precise card chosen at random by someone with you in the bar.

Shuffle a pack of cards and ask your friend to choose one and to place it face up on the table. Then phone your friend (who has already been prepped) and ask, 'Hi, is [insert friend's name] there please?' Your friend responds by slowly saying 'clubs, hearts, diamonds, spades', while you pretend to wait for your friend to come to the phone. When he or she reaches the correct suit, you interrupt by saying 'Ah, hi [insert friend's name], can you identify a card for me?' Your friend quickly replies 'ace, two, three, four, five …' and when s/he reaches the correct number, you interrupt with, 'Thanks, I'll pass you over'. Then switch to speakerphone so that your long-distance friend can correctly identify your bemused victim's card.

A bacon sandwich walks into a bar. 'I'm sorry, madam,' says the bartender, 'but we don't serve food'.

"A strong drink can numb the soul as good as any prayer."

ERIN BOWMAN, *VENGEANCE ROAD*

HOW QUICKLY
Does my Liver
RECOVER?

If you're a heavy drinker and you haven't been to the doctor recently for a health check and blood test, it's easy to worry that your habits may have caught up with you.

The good news is that the liver is one hell of an organ; it takes a lot of punishment to destroy it beyond repair, and it can recover quickly.

The bad news is that once you start to experience any symptoms – yellowish tint to your skin especially under your fingernails, yellow eyes (due to the accumulation of bilirubin in the blood), spots, chronic fatigue, persistent diarrhoea, itchy skin, weight loss, dark urine, pale stools, bloody or black stools, bruising easily, nausea and loss of appetite, dull pain in the upper-right area of the abdomen just below the ribs – the damage is already done, the liver is slowly failing and it may be too late to make a full recovery.

Regardless of whether or not you're experiencing any of these symptoms, if you know you're a problem drinker, get yourself down to your doctor and ask for a health check. You may be relieved to find that your blood results are normal, and that may encourage you to reduce your drinking, in the knowledge that you haven't passed the point of no return. Or you could take the all-clear as a sign that you can continue to thrash your body's second biggest organ for another 10 years.

Sadly, just because you don't need a liver transplant yet doesn't mean that you can continue to persecute the one you were born with, because it does so much more than simply carry away waste from the body. In fact, the liver performs more than 500 vital functions, including: production of certain proteins for blood plasma, making and balancing glucose levels, making immune factors and removing bacteria from the bloodstream, regulating blood levels of amino acids, storing iron, converting poisonous ammonia to urea and regulating blood clotting.

So, as you reach for another drink, maybe stop thinking of your liver through the binary construct of healthy/screwed (which in itself is probably a sign that you have an unhealthy relationship with alcohol). Any reduction in your drinking will have significant health benefits and improve your liver function.

HOW TO

*** *Bullshit* ***

ABOUT WINE

The Romans knew a thing or two about wine, and they invented one of its first aphorisms: *In vino veritas* (in wine lies the truth), meaning that drunk people lose their inhibitions.

It's hardly the most profound observation ever made about the effects of alcohol on the prefrontal cortex, but it persists because it's written in a foreign language and sounds clever.

That sums up the entire wine industry, or rather, the culture of rubbish that surrounds it, because the truth is, nobody really knows what they're talking about. Studies show that wine experts can give wildly different ratings to the same wine, they can't tell the difference between red and white (when they can't see the colour) and in blind tests they've failed to distinguish a Chateau Lafite from a litre of Slovakian antifreeze.

'I know what I like' is as profound in its honesty as 'I love the generous and layered aromas of boysenberry and smoky dark chocolate'. But the thing about the fermented grape is that if you want to sound cultured, you have to throw around some adjectives and learn the names of some obscure aromas associated with each type of wine. For instance, if you can detect mushroom, leather, pheasant, truffle or wet leaves in your Pinot Noir, you display a fine nose, even if the wine cost less than a fiver and is unlikely to show any of that subtlety.

Here's a quick reference guide to the major grape varieties. All you have to do is know which grape you're drinking, then use the rubbish phrases associated with it.

CABERNET SAUVIGNON dark red colour, robust full-bodied, medium to high tannins and medium acidity; dark fruit, black cherry, blackcurrant, liquorice, black olive, vanilla, oak, jammy, black pepper, bell pepper, tobacco, leather, violets, rose, cassis, truffle

USE THE RUBBISH PHRASES

CHARDONNAY oaked/unoaked, buttery or crisp, zesty lemon (less ripe) or more tropical fruit flavours, vanilla notes, oily, butterscotch, freshness, acidity, minerality

CHENIN BLANC medium to high acidity; passion fruit, crisp apple, pear, peach, lemon, quince, ginger, chamomile, honeysuckle, jasmine, mango, butterscotch, marzipan

GEWÜRZTRAMINER grapefruit, lychee, pineapple depending on ripeness, cat wee (cheap), rose petal, ginger, lemon oil, cloves, cinnamon, honey, sweet smoky incense

GRENACHE Light, cherry-red colour, semi-translucent; medium tannins and acidity; strawberry, raspberry, oak ageing for toasty cinnamon, anise, slatey minerality

MALBEC deep purple-red colour, magenta-tinged rim, dark fruit-forward, medium tannin and acidity; red cherry, raspberry, blackberry, black cherry, plum, violet, chocolate, cocoa powder, leather, sweet tobacco

MERLOT dark purplish-red colour, medium tannin, medium acidity; plummy, velvety, blackberry, chocolate, liquorice, mocha, black cherry, jam, vanilla, oak, nutmeg, coffee, cinnamon, chocolate, truffle, wet earth, fresh flowers

MUSCAT/MOSCATO primary flavours of peach, orange, nectarine; mint, rosewood, citrus fruits, birch trees

NEBBIOLO brick-red, translucent, orange rim; full-bodied flavour with high tannin and acidity; roses, violets, autumn leaves, cherry, raspberry, cranberry, fruit cake, clove, anise, leather, wood smoke, tar, red clay

PINOT GRIGIO crisp, tangy dryness and high acidity; lime, lemon, pear, nectarine, apple, honeysuckle, spicy almond, salty minerality

PINOT NOIR pale, translucent colour; low to moderate tannin, crisp acidity; silky, satin, raspberry, cranberry, black cherry and strawberry, violet, rose petals, mushroom, leather, game, truffle, wet leaves, mint

RIESLING nectarine, apricot, apple, lime peel, honey, jasmine, kerosene

SANGIOVESE maroon/blood-red colour, high tannin and acidity; violet, cherry, redcurrant, strawberry, fig, roasted pepper, tomato, dark chocolate, leather, tobacco, oregano, roses, light oak

SAUVIGNON BLANC green herbaceous flavours, razor-sharp dryness, medium-high acidity; zesty lime, crisp green apple, peach, bell pepper, grass, fennel, gooseberry, grapefruit, lemon, herbs

SÉMILLON medium to low acidity; zippy lemon, fresh apple, pear, papaya, mango, waxy taste, honeysuckle, saffron, hay, ginger, buttery oak

SYRAH deep red-purple colour, pink at the rim, medium tannins and acidity; blackberry, blueberry, peppery finish, oak, olive, clove, vanilla, mint, liquorice, chocolate, bacon, grilled meat, leather, smoke, tobacco

TEMPRANILLO medium ruby to medium garnet colour, translucent, medium tannin and acidity; cherry, plum, tomato, dried fig, leather, tobacco, cedar, vanilla

VIOGNIER full-bodied white wine; peach, tangerine, honeysuckle, creamy vanilla, nutmeg, clove, almond

ZINFANDEL deep red, translucent, medium-high tannin and acidity; spice, candied fruit flavour, strawberry, blackberry, cloves, cinnamon, liquorice, mocha, sweet tobacco, smoky

A neutron walks into a bar and orders a drink and a packet of crisps. 'How much do I owe you?' the neutron asks the bartender. 'For you, no charge.'

"If your arteries are good, eat more ice cream. If they are bad, drink more red wine. Proceed thusly."

SANDRA BYRD, *BON APPETIT*

Drink
TEQUILA
Like a Mexican

Tequila is a type of mezcal, which is a distilled alcoholic beverage made from any type of agave.

Tequila is made from the large succulent blue agave plant (aka *Agave tequilana*), primarily in the area surrounding the Mexican city of Tequila and in the Jaliscan Highlands (Los Altos de Jalisco). It has an unfair reputation of being a hardcore drink that will quickly send you under the table, but that's because outside of Mexico, tequila shots are consumed by people who are already drunk off their face, so it gets the blame for ensuing stomach pumping/alcohol coma/ massive hangover.

In reality, the only truly hardcore fact about tequila is that the flowers of the blue agave plant are pollinated by the greater long-nosed bat. Each plant produces several thousand seeds, but many of them are sterile. There's a metaphor in there somewhere, if you can bother to unpick it.

The tequila worm or scorpion are also misconceptions. Only a few mezcals come with a worm/scorpion in the bottle (*con gusano/escorpión*) and this is not a Mexican tradition, it's just a marketing ploy, designed to challenge the machismo of stupid party animals. Even the worm isn't a worm, it's the larval form of the moth Hypopta agavis, which lives on the agave plant. Finding these larvae in a batch of agave plants is bad news for a brewer.

To do a slammer, lick the back of your hand below the index finger, pour on some salt (it sticks to where you licked), then lick the salt off your hand, drink the tequila and then quickly suck on a wedge of lemon or lime.

If you really want to consume tequila like a Mexican, don't dress it up – drink it neat. That's all. The salt and lime ritual has grown up purely to lessen the burning sensation, and the sour fruit enhances the flavour, but if you think doing tequila slammers makes you edgy or part of the frat pack, you're sadly deluded.

Why Dry January is an AWFUL IDEA

If you're one of those drinkers who tries to make up for Christmas holiday overindulgence by doing 'Dry January' then you could be doing yourself more harm than good, according to leading health experts.

Millions of people around the world abstain from alcohol for the first month of the year, but according to doctor Mark Wright, a consultant at University Hospital Southampton in the UK, many abstainers compensate for their January sobriety by binge drinking guilt-free for the rest of the year.

Dr Wright says 'Giving up alcohol for Dry January as some sort of detox is like maxing out your credit cards all year and then thinking you can solve your financial problems by living like a hermit for a month'. This all-or-nothing approach is typical of heavy drinkers. In fact, one of the signs of problem drinking is repeatedly trying and failing to set temporary limits on your intake. In any case, a month is too short a time to change your habit (wet blanket psychologists estimate that it takes on average 66 days to form a new habit).

While ditching the booze may be good for your finances, it may impact both your business and social lives, and there's no clinical proof that a month of abstinence has any major benefits. There's just one study carried out by the editorial team of *New Scientist* with 10 volunteers who quit alcohol for a month and lowered their cholesterol, blood glucose levels and fat around the liver. They also reported improved sleep and concentration. But 10 is a tiny sample, so if you want the scientific proof, you'll be pleased to learn that the jury is still out. Besides, if you're a hard drinker, a month off won't repair the liver damage of thirty years of heavy drinking, and your other organs – heart, brain, pancreas – will need even more time to recover than your liver; and if you're a sensible drinker, your organs won't need a one-month sabbatical anyway.

If you're not going to quit altogether, your best long-term strategy, as recommended by whining medical professionals, is to have two or three alcohol-free days a week, all year round.

***
TEN REASONS
BEER IS GOOD FOR YOU

Lots of research supports the benefits of drinking beer in moderation

So long as you can limit yourself to one pint a day (14 units a week), you can improve your health in many ways from preventing heart attacks, Alzheimer's and diabetes to reducing inflammation, boosting your immune system, brain and protecting your lungs.

Sadly, if you drink more than this amount, according to killjoy scientists in cahoots with the nanny state, you will lose the benefits and increase your risk of a variety of ailments. Who the hell drinks just one pint of beer a day? Reactionaries in crimson chinos living in languorous moderation, so it's no wonder they outlive most of the interesting hellraisers who grab life by the balls and party hard.

1. Protects your lungs: a 2007 study by the American College of Chest Physicians found that moderate drinkers performed better on breathing tests than teetotallers, and that drinking fewer than two drinks a day can reduce lung disease by 20 per cent. Japanese scientists also discovered the protective properties of hops, which contains a chemical compound called humulone which protects against the respiratory syncytial virus, and is anti-inflammatory.

2. Lowers blood pressure: drinking too much alcohol can raise blood pressure to unhealthy levels, but moderate beer drinking reduces it, as shown by a Nurses Health study involving 70,000 women aged 25 to 42. The study found that women who drank moderate amounts of beer had lower blood pressure than those who drank moderate amounts of wine or spirits.

3. Reduces the risk of Alzheimer's: two recent studies, one from the University of Lanzhou, China, the other from the University of Rochester, point towards the protective qualities of the antioxidants contained in beer (specifically hops), that reduce brain inflammation and flush out the toxins associated with cognitive decline.

The Chinese scientists found an ingredient in hops, called xanthohumol, which protects brain cells from the oxidative damage associated with dementia. Once again, studies in mice annoyingly found that overindulgence has the opposite effect.

4. Reduces the risk of diabetes: moderate beer drinking helps to regulate blood sugar levels, and reduces the insulin resistance and the risk of diabetes, according to research published by the European Association for the Study of Diabetes. This research showed that people who drink three to four times per week are less prone to diabetes than teetotallers. Another study from Harokopio University in Athens with 1,500 men linked low daily intake of beer with a halved risk of diabetes.

5. Protects your heart and blood vessels: a meta-study of 150 studies, carried out by the IRCCS Mediterranean Neurological Institute in Pozzilli, Italy, found that a daily pint of beer can reduce the risk of heart disease by a third. Once again this is thought to be linked to beer's antioxidants. Plus its beneficial mineral content which includes phosphorus, iodine, magnesium and potassium.

6. Increases bone density: a 2010 study by the Department of Food Science & Technology at the University of California, identified malted barley and hops in beer as a significant source of dietary silicon, a key ingredient for

increasing bone mineral density and in the formation of connective tissue.

7. Boosts your brain: this same dietary silicon helps to protect the brain against the build-up of harmful compounds that cause mental decline.

8. Beer is anti-inflammatory: inflammation is one of the key causes and indicators of disease, so anything that has anti-inflammatory properties is generally well received. Recent sports research into endurance athletes has linked the higher IBU (International Bitterness Units) found in the stronger IPAs (India pale ales) with higher anti-inflammatory properties, contained in its polyphenols (anti-oxidants). But sadly, these were alcohol-free beverages.

9. Protects your kidneys: scientists from Finland found that each beer reduces a man's risk of developing kidney stones by 40 per cent. This may simply be because of the increased fluid consumption or because the hops in beer may slow the release of calcium in the body, which is the building material for kidney stones.

10. Contains nutrients: especially B vitamins, which are often deficient in chronic drinkers. B vitamin deficiency in excessive drinkers is associated with a wide range of diseases involving the nervous system, heart, skin, bone marrow and gastrointestinal system.

Brandy is made by distilling wine, which is then aged in an oak barrel.

There are many ways to drink brandy, but a basic rule would be that if it's quality brandy, savour it neat; if it's cheaper stuff, mix it with anything: soda water, tonic, ginger ale, soda or make a cocktail like a Sidecar.

The quickest way to tell the quality of brandy (apart from tasting it) is to see how long it's been aged, because ageing costs money and inferior quality brandy isn't worth the effort and expense. Here's the age rating system for brandies, which is a rough guide for cost and quality:

AC: aged for at least two years in a barrel

VS: 'Very Special' – aged for a minimum of three years in a barrel

VSOP: 'Very Superior Old Pale' – aged for a minimum of five years in a barrel

XO: 'Extra Old', Napoleon or Vieille Reserve – aged for a minimum of six years in a barrel

Vintage: aged in the barrel and marked with a single year (i.e. not blended with brandy from other years)

Hors D'age: 'beyond age' – aged for 30 years and above in a barrel

The classic way to enjoy a well-aged quality brandy is in a brandy snifter, which you cup in the palm of your hand for several minutes to gently warm the brandy and release its aromas. These aromas are concentrated by the spacious bowl but trapped by the tapered rim, which should still be wide enough for you to stick your nose in. A young brandy will have sharp, fruity and floral notes with a hint of spice; older brandies have a complex aroma, with softer fruit but plenty of spice, and subtle notes of vanilla and nuttiness.

Brandy and cognac aren't interchangeable terms. Cognac comes from one region of southwest France, primarily from ugni blanc grapes, and is distilled twice and aged in barrels made from French oak.

Newbies should kick-off with the four major brands: Hennessy, Courvoisier, Rémy Martin and Martell, which have all been producing the stuff since the eighteenth century.

Is Methylated Spirit *REALLY* * *THAT BAD FOR YOU?*

Before we discuss the merits and pitfalls of drinking methylated spirit, let's kick off with a simple warning: don't drink it.

Even if you believe in Multiverse Theory, there's no scenario in any of the possible universes in which drinking meths ends well for you, OK? Let's just put that out there before we have some fun by asking 'what if?'

Methylated spirit, aka denatured alcohol, is ethanol (drinking alcohol) with additives that make it poisonous and bitter-tasting to discourage people from drinking it. It is often dyed purple to highlight its toxicity. The additives usually depend on its specific industrial use, but the main additive has traditionally been at least 10 per cent methanol, and other typical additives include acetone, isopropyl alcohol, methyl ethyl ketone, methyl isobutyl ketone and bitter-tasting denatonium. In some countries, such as the USA, the per centage of methanol (and its corresponding toxicity) is often much higher.

Take a Shot

If you were to drink a shot glass of neat methanol, initially you'd experience less severe symptoms of intoxication than if you'd downed an identical amount of ethanol, but the real damage would be done when your body broke down the methanol into formaldehyde (embalming fluid) and then into formic acid (stinging nettles/ant venom). To oversimplify to make it sound more interesting: this would turn your blood into acid and screw up your body cells at the mitochondrial level (that's really bad).

Apart from the vomiting and abdominal pain, your kidneys would pack in and you'd also go blind over a number of hours and then die. Ironically, if you drink ethanol first, this reduces the toxicity of the methanol, because it prevents the body from breaking it down, so it's excreted intact by the kidneys. But hang on ... methanol and ethanol combined is … methylated spirit. So has everyone been lying about its poisonous effects?

Just don't go there. There are better ways of kicking against the nanny state than drinking meths. If you run out of booze, mouthwash and hand sanitiser on the same afternoon, and are tempted to hit the purple stuff, remind yourself of this joke: two guys are sitting in the park one afternoon with a huge bottle of meths because they want to get completely wasted. The first guy takes a giant slug and then says to his buddy, 'Let's drink faster, it's getting dark already!'.

A dog walks into a bar. The barman says, 'Excuse me, but whose dog is this? The sign outside clearly says NO DOGS ALLOWED'. The dog says, 'Well, I'm not just any dog you know'. The barman sniffs. 'So what makes you so special?' The dog sits down and replies wearily, 'Just think about what's happening right now. Take your time. I've got all day'.

"*I mostly drink clear booze because the rest of it looks as if it's already been through a gentleman.*"

CHRISTOPHER BUEHLMAN,
THOSE ACROSS THE RIVER

SEVEN HANGOVER MYTHS
You Have Got to
STOP BELIEVING

It's a revealing characteristic of humankind that we expend so much effort devising new ways to cure morning hangovers – an entirely self-inflicted problem – instead of taking personal responsibility for the night before.

There's no escaping the fact that a night on the lash messes up your brain chemicals and hammers the central nervous system. Everyone who has ever had a drink knows the symptoms: headache, nausea, dodgy stomach, self-loathing, abject dehydration.

Hangover symptoms can really only be fixed by time, fluids and a good night's sleep, but here are some popular but ultimately unworthy challengers for the eternally vacant title of Hangover Cure.

1. **'Lining' your stomach.** Biologically, there's no such thing as 'lining your stomach', which already has its own effective lining of mucus secreted through thousands of tiny pores called gastric pits. These pits also squirt out digestive enzymes and hydrochloric acid to digest whatever you put in your mouth. Some people believe that a pint of milk, or a few chugs of olive oil, line the stomach and protect them from a hangover. Fatty foods will marginally slow down the rate at which the stomach empties, but only 20 per cent of alcohol is absorbed through the stomach; the rest passes into the small intestine.

2. **Hair of the dog.** One of the signs of problem drinking is that you need an alcoholic drink in the morning to help you to function or to 'cure' your hangover. It comes from the idea that the cause of an ailment can also be its cure – this is the basis for vaccination, but a hangover is neither viral nor bacterial. Hangover symptoms are worse when all the alcohol has left your body, so having a morning drink may postpone the inevitable and boost endorphins (the body's natural painkillers), but the hangover will return when you sober up again.

CAUSE OF AN AILMENT CAN ALSO BE ITS CURE?

3. **Two aspirin and a glass of water before bed.** Dehydration is one of the factors that create a hangover, so a large glass of water before bed is a good idea; aspirin is anti-inflammatory, so it will supply marginal benefits, but neither will provide magic protection against the other causes of a hangover such as low blood sugar, poor sleep and loss of electrolytes.

4. **A greasy spoon fried breakfast.** When you're hung over, your body needs simple carbohydrates that it can digest quickly to raise your blood sugar levels. A fatty cooked breakfast takes longer to digest, and doesn't 'soak up' the alcohol (which has already been absorbed into the bloodstream). Here are some better alternatives:

   - water, water, water
   - water-rich fruits: melon, grapefruit and oranges to hydrate, they'll also provide a quick energy source and replenish vitamins
   - Greek yogurt topped with berries: the lactobacillus bacteria helps to reduce gut inflammation; the berries supply a quick source of energy
   - green tea: full of antioxidants and water, and helps to stabilise blood sugar levels
   - peppermint tea: soothes your digestive tract
   - small omelette: eggs contain the amino acid cysteine, which breaks down the acetaldehyde in your system

- banana: a quick source of energy that helps to restore levels of potassium.

5. **Strong cup of black coffee.** Coffee will help to hydrate you (caffeine is a diuretic but you still gain more water than you lose), and it may make you feel more alert, but it won't help you process the alcohol any quicker, and if you have a queasy stomach, its acidity may make it worse. Also, if you drink too much coffee, you'll add twitchy restlessness to your growing list of hangover symptoms.

6. **Carb-loading before bed.** Eating any food will slow the rate of absorption of any remaining alcohol in your stomach, so by all means eat some carbs if that's what you crave. But try to avoid acidic, spicy or salty food, which may cause indigestion or acid reflux (stomach acid flows back up into the food pipe and makes you choke). If you eat too much of anything, it will disrupt the quality of your sleep and worsen your hangover.

7. **Throwing up.** If you throw up naturally, that will have the beneficial effect of getting rid of the alcohol still in your stomach. However, you shouldn't make yourself sick because this puts a lot of pressure on your oesophagus. Habitual self-induced vomiting could lead to oesophageal tears (called Mallory-Weiss tears) and make you puke blood.

BREW YOUR OWN

Hooch

If you find yourself doing hard time in prison, boarding school or seminary, or you just enjoy really rough tasting liquor, brewing your own hooch, chalk, buck, juice, pruno – whatever you want to call it – is a good way to gain a disappointing, retch-inducing buzz for a few hours, or to sell to fellow inmates/pupils/seminarians.

Here's a traditional recipe that's been used in numerous prisons for decades.

Peel 10 oranges and throw them into a heavy-duty garden rubbish bag with the contents of a small tin of fruit cocktail. Seal the bag tightly, then mash the fruit together with your hands until it becomes a mushy paste, then open the bag, add half a litre of warm (not hot) tap water and reseal. Soak the bag in a sink full of warm water for 15 minutes, then wrap in towels or sheets to keep some of the heat in, and stash your bag in a dark place where the prying eyes of authority can't find it.

Two days later, carefully open up the bag, which should be puffed up with lots of carbon dioxide (produced by fermentation), throw in about 150g of sugar (that's about 50 sugar cubes, if you've been stealing supplies from the refectory) and 6 sachets of tomato sauce. Reseal the bag, knead the pulp again to help dissolve the sugar, give the bag another soak in a sink full of warm water for half an hour, then wrap it up again and leave it in your dark hiding place for another week.

Within a few days, your concoction should smell of rotting fruit and there'll be plenty of mould floating around too. It will look like a blocked sewer that needs power hosing. Each day, release the carbon dioxide and warm up the bag in the sink for half an hour.

After a total of 10 days, strain the mixture through a cotton T-shirt or sock, and your incarceration wine is ready to drink. Well … not ready, just available. You might consider adding some meths (see page 70) to make it more palatable. If 10 days is too long to wait to poison yourself, add a few slices of mashed-up bread to the mix on the first day to speed up the process.

Downing four pints of ale from a beautifully crafted horn-shaped 'ell glass' – dignity intact – as your ugly friends loudly chant your name, may be tempting; but learning how to get all that amber nectar down your throat rather than your Ben Sherman shirt actually requires a smattering of technique.

The fact that you seek knowledge from a book, rather than down your local, speaks volumes about the vanilla company you keep. But don't despair – sometimes a little book-learning will take you further than the dubious goading of your sottish companions.

But first, some history. The ell glass takes its name from the 'ell' – a measurement of one yard and nine inches. The yard of ale was especially popular in English taverns during the seventeenth century, and legend has it that its proportions enabled highwaymen sitting atop horse-drawn carriages to quench their thirst without having to disembark. Which begs the question: how did they wee?

Spillage, the bane of all newbie ell glass bibbers, can be avoided by understanding that tilting too far allows air to reach the bulbous bottom of the glass, releasing a tidal wave of ale held in place by an airlock. Here's how to prevent this embarrassment by controlling the flow:

1. Hold the neck of the glass in your left hand (right if you're left-handed) and fully extend your other arm along the length of the glass. The longer your reach, the greater will be your control of the glass (it's all about leverage).

2. To prevent an ale rush, lift and tilt the glass slowly as you drink and twist so that air reaches the bottom gradually.

3. Some drinkers twirl the glass quickly, to create a vortex that uses centrifugal force to keep the ale at the outside of the glass so that it slides down the throat more easily.

4. Raise the empty vessel aloft, utter a hearty roar and hold up your other hand for the volley of high fives that will doubtless rain down to crown your triumph.

HOW
*** Bartenders ***
STEAL FROM
CUSTOMERS

Bartending is hard work; it involves dealing with more arseholes than a proctologist, only with longer hours and for considerably less money.

Most bartenders are honest, and are just trying to get through another shift without losing their sanity. But there are a few who use a repertoire of tricks to fleece unwary customers.

Here are seven common scams:

1. The oldest fiddle is the short pour – measuring less spirit than the customer has paid for, then repeating as necessary so the measures add up during a stock take. Sometimes, a drinking straw or the rim of the glass is coated in the spirit to disguise the short pour.

2. When a bartender pours a shot from the bottle (rather than use an optic), when he raises the bottle mid-pour to create a long stream of liquid, this not only looks flash, but it can disguise a short pour, because a long stream of liquid always looks like a generous measure.

3. Another way to make a normal measure appear more generous is to add extra ice and go short on the mixer, which fools the customer with a stronger taste, and also means they finish their drink more quickly.

4. When a customer asks for a shot of spirits, without naming a specific brand or price band, this allows plenty of scope for the bartender to up sell by reaching for a premium product, which can cost several times more than the entry-level stuff.

    HOW TO IDENTIFY A SHORT POUR

5. Conversely, some establishments will add some of the cheap stuff to a top

shelf bottle, and it can be hard to detect once a mixer such as Red Bull or Coke has been added. If you want to splash your cash drink it neat so you can establish the quality.

6. In countries like the USA where tipping is expected, check that it isn't automatically included on the bill, otherwise you'll end up tipping twice.

7. When a bartender goes above and beyond to give you a really good service and makes you feel like you're their best and most liked customer, they may be scamming you to get a bigger tip. Even when you know they're faking it, it's their job to make sure you have a good time, so should you cut them some slack for their transparently artless hustle, or only reward servers who have a naturally likeable personality? That's a tough call.

A wall walks into a bar and orders a drink. 'I'm sorry, sir, but I'm not allowed to serve you.' 'Why not?' asks the wall. 'You're plastered.'

"*This is turning into an alcohol-will-cure-everything kind of day.*"

KELLY MORAN, *BEWITCHED*

✳ ✳ ✳
COCKTAILS
ARE FOR IDIOTS

Why is it that certain sectors of society can only enjoy themselves by wasting their cash, braying loudly to their friends and making life unpleasant for everybody else?

In a crowded bar, their favourite way to tighten every sphincter in the room – apart from exuding toxic levels of self-entitlement and talking endlessly about their bonuses – is to order a large round of complicated cocktails that will tie up a bartender for the next half hour. Then after two sips, the cocktail's been shot-gunned and it's the turn of another preening gel-haired popped-collared wannabe Gatsby to get a round in. Idiots.

Fashions and fads come and go, so it's difficult to be definitive about which cocktails are the most idiot-ish. Even that bastion of gracious debate – the Internet – can't agree. If you Google 'Cocktails only idiots would order' one web scribe who's a self-confessed 'consummate foodie, awesome girlfriend, major appliance owner and cat person', claims that ordering an Old Fashioned is an idiot move 'because they know it's a pain in the arse to prepare – there's a sugar cube and muddling involved'; strawberry daiquiris are a waste of the minuscule amounts of alcohol they contain; and demanding 'a top-shelf, dirty martini' means paying too much for quality gin/vodka hashed up with 'stale, filthy olive garnish brine-water'. Finally, frozen virgin drinks of any kind require a blender, so they're time-consuming and don't even get you drunk. However, another Internet opinion is that Old Fashioned is 'one of the easiest drinks' to make. Ask for one at your local and make your own mind up.

Here are the basic idiot cocktail principles that survive the test of time: faddy, complicated to prepare, display an ignorance about the quality of ingredients, require sullying of ingredients just to hit a trend or contain no alcohol. But ultimately, when an idiot orders a cocktail, de facto it becomes an idiot cocktail.

Stop WETTING the Bed

Bedwetting while asleep is called 'nocturnal enuresis' and it's more common among adults than you might imagine.

According to research published in the *British Medical Journal* in 2013, between 0.5 and 2 per cent of adults involuntarily wet the bed in their sleep. You can probably double that figure, since lots of people don't admit to having this problem.

It's bad enough having to change the sheets in the middle of the night, and mortifying if you're sharing the bed with someone else (although, if it happens in a hotel –

winning!) Fortunately, if this is you, you can do something about it, and it doesn't happen just because of the amount of liquid you've consumed, although that's a factor. The alcohol alters the function of an important hormone in your body, and it also irritates the muscles in your bladder.

ALCOHOL IRRITATES THE MUSCLES IN YOUR BLADDER

Watch the Damp Patch

The hormone in question is called antidiuretic hormone (ADH), which is manufactured by special nerve cells in the hypothalamus, which is located at the base of the brain and released into the bloodstream via the nearby pituitary gland. The ADH regulates the fluid volume in your body by controlling the amount of water in the urine, because it can tell the kidneys to take back water from the urine so that it can return to the bloodstream.

Normally, as you become more dehydrated, your urine becomes more yellow-brown and concentrated. However, alcohol disrupts this process by suppressing the release of ADH, so your kidneys stop reabsorbing water and it fills up your bladder instead, even though you might be drinking shorts rather than pints of beer. So when you ingest alcohol, you become dehydrated because you wee more, regardless of the volume of water in your drink.

This suppression of ADH continues through the night while you're asleep, so your body will continue to produce more urine than if you were sober. Alcohol makes you sleep more deeply during the first half of the night, so where a full bladder would normally wake you up, drunks are more difficult to rouse.

An added complication is that the walls of the bladder are mainly formed from smooth detrusor muscle, which contracts to release urine from the bladder when you wee. Alcohol irritates this muscle and makes it contract, so even if you aren't bursting for a piss, alcohol can still make you slash like a Siberian Husky while you blithely dream you're floating on a raft with Ryan Reynolds/ Chris Hemsworth or Scarlett Johansson. Take your pick.

So how can you reduce the risk of waking up in an ochre oasis? Drink less fluid, drink less alcohol and avoid caffeine (ditch the Red Bull mixers and late-night cups of coffee) which also irritates the bladder's detrusor muscle. If it happens frequently, visit a doctor to rule out other urological issues, and invest in a mattress protector and a catheter.

> **A bartender says, 'We don't serve time travellers in here.' A time traveller walks into a bar.**

DRINK *Like a* PSYCHOPATH

There's been a lot of buzz recently about two studies published in 2016, in the journal *Appetite* by Christina Sagioglou and Tobias Greitemeyer from the University of Innsbruck in Austria.

Previous studies have shown that people with increased preferences for sweet foods were more likely to be agreeable and neurotic, and have linked bitter taste preference to harsher moral judgments and increased hostility. The researchers in Austria widened their focus to include sweet, sour, salty and bitter.

In the first study, researchers surveyed 500 adults and asked them about their preferences for four types of foods: sweet, sour, salty and bitter, and they assessed them with four different personality tests. In the second study, the researchers also asked participants to rate the sweetness, sourness, saltiness and bitterness of various foods, to assess whether they agreed those foods belonged in their categories.

A Bitter Taste

According to the abstract, 'The results of both studies confirmed the hypothesis that bitter taste preferences are positively associated with malevolent personality traits, with the most robust relation to everyday sadism and psychopathy ... consistently demonstrating a robust relation between increased enjoyment of bitter foods and heightened sadistic proclivities'. In the first experiment, bitter taste preference was also linked to narcissism and Machiavellianism.

Tell us something we don't know. Catherine the Great was famously a lover of cruciferous vegetables and drinking the blood of virgins, while Vlad the Impaler liked nothing better than snacking on dandelion greens and chugging apple cider vinegar.

Steven Meyers, PhD, professor of psychology at Roosevelt University, disagrees. He reviewed the Innsbruck studies for *Health* magazine and claims that he found in the study only a 'very small association' between taste preference and personality traits. He advises caution when interpreting the results, and says they need to be replicated by other scientists. But since when did narcissistic psychopaths approach anything with caution? You have to ask yourself, WWDTD (What would Donald Trump Drink?).

TRUMP CLAIMS TO BE A PROUD TEETOTALLER

In fact, Trump claims to be a proud teetotaller who has never had a drink, smoked cigarettes or taken drugs. But that's because he's a self-confessed control freak who is terrified of losing his judgement and his inhibitions. Tim O'Brien, author of the biography *TrumpNation* explains, 'I think he's scared of the effects alcohol can have on people because he witnessed first-hand how it destroyed his brother's life, and I think he's a teetotaller because he's scared of it in himself'.

So there you have it. If you like a black coffee, bitter IPAs and Gin and Tonic, and always order a bitter Negroni cocktail when it's happy hour, you're probably a narcissistic psychopath who likes to manipulate and take advantage of others to achieve your goals. Going teetotal won't help you to hide.

* Five Ultra-Gnarly *
BEERS TO TRY
BEFORE YOU DIE

The Urban Dictionary defines gnarly as 'when you've gone beyond radical, beyond extreme, it's balls-out danger, and/or perfection, and/or skill, or all of that combined'.

Ergo, 'ultra-gnarly' must be like when you reach the edge of the extreme skill universe and puke into the abyss, dude. These five beers are so rad that their descriptions alone can make people blow chunks.

1. **Big Konas, Perrin Microbrewery, ABV: 7.4%.** An American Brown Ale-style beer brewed in a limited 30-barrel batch by Perrin Microbrewery, using coffee

beans that have been eaten and defecated by civet cats. The coffee beans are so rare and expensive that the brewer had to wait six months and endure many interviews before he was given permission to use the product. You can only sample the beer onsite in 8-ounce pours at the brewery in Comstock Park, Michigan, USA, if it hasn't already been retired.

2. **Hvalur 2, Steðji Microbrewery, ABV: 5.2 per cent.** This Porter-like Icelandic brew is made during the winter months from pure glacial water, malted barley, hops and ... sheep-crap-smoked whale balls. One giant Fin whale nad (the size of a basketball and weighing about 8kg) is used for each batch of beer, but first it's chopped up and cured according to an old Icelandic tradition, salted and smoked with sheep dung. This gnarly nadger brew goes down an arctic storm at local food festivals, forming the perfect accompaniment to dishes such as boiled sheep heads, ram testicles, wind-dried fish and fermented shark.

3. **Beard Beer, Rogue Ales, ABV: 5.6 per cent.** This American wild ale is brewed in Newport, Oregon, USA, using wild yeast originally cultured from nine hairs from the beard of Rogue Ales' brewmaster, John Maier. When the beer went on sale on April 1, 2013, *The Oregonian* newspaper thought it was an April Fools prank. It has a hazy orange hue and a sweet bready taste with a notable

pineapple flavour. Daniel Tapper from *The Guardian* detected notes of banana and passion fruit, and described it as 'the weirdest beer I've ever tried'.

4. **Chicha, Dogfish Head Brewery, ABV: 3.1 per cent.** This ancient beer is brewed with malted corn and barley, plus Peruvian purple maize that's been chewed in the actual mouths of hundreds of Dogfish co-workers (according to their website, at their annual Hootenanny, 'hundreds of co-workers gathered ... In the ultimate spirit of teamwork, each person was given a cup of purple corn to chew up and spit out to contribute to the brewing ingredients'). The wort is then boiled, chilled, blended with strawberries and fermented.

5. **The End of History, BrewDog, ABV: 55 per cent.** Brewed by a Scottish company just outside of Columbus, Ohio, USA, this ultra-limited blond Belgian ale is one of the strongest and most expensive beers you'll ever buy (if you can get your hands on a bottle – originally it was only offered to shareholders who stumped up a $20,000 investment). The BrewDog website claims it has 'torn up convention, blurred distinctions and pushed brewing to its absolute limits' and describes the beer as 'a perfect conceptual marriage between art, taxidermy and craft brewing'. Taxidermy? Oh, did we forget to mention that each bottle is wrapped in a dead squirrel?